DEDICATION

This book is dedicated to all
Entrepreneurs, who have the courage
to strike out on their own in pursuit of
financial freedom and lasting security
despite the critics, who themselves have neither.

HOW TO SLAY THE FINANCIAL DRAGON
Winning the Battle for Time and Money

William A. Stanmeyer, JD

HOW TO SLAY THE FINANCIAL DRAGON
Winning the Battle for Time and Money

The information given in this book is general financial comment and is not to be construed as specific advice to the reader on his or her financial position. Such advice should be sought only from a qualified person whose professional training or personal achievements demonstrate a high level of financial acumen and skill as a financial service professional or as a successful entrepreneur, and who is aware of all pertinent facts and circumstances in the reader's situation.

This book is published by: The J&W Business Group, P.O. Box 15, Great Falls VA 22066. Phone: (703) 749-3214

Printed in the United States of America by Good Printers, Inc., Bridgewater, Virginia.

First Edition, October 2002.

ISBN: 0-9650992-2-9

TABLE OF CONTENTS

CHAPTER I: THE HERO AND THE DRAGON

"Personal debt has given America three distinct classes of people: the Haves, the Have-Nots, and the Haven't-Paid-for-What-They-Haves."

– Anonymous

* * * * * * * *

The Hero and the Dragon

Often in ancient myths, a Dragon attacked the Hero. He had a strong arm and a mighty sword. Like a meat-eating dinosaur, the Dragon breathed fire and had huge teeth. For bad measure, often it had many heads. This was a Hydra.

The agile Hero dodged the hungry reptile and sliced off a head. But out popped *two more* in its place! He swung his mighty sword again and severed another head; but then *two more grew out* in place of the one just cut off! His very success made things worse!

A battle like this cannot go on for long. As it gains more new heads all weaving and lunging, the Hydra is sure to singe the Hero. Or eat him. He must change tactics quickly.

You know how it ends. The Hero changes his target; he stops cutting necks. Instead, he dodges some flames and *plunges his sword into the monster's heart.*

This story is a parable, stretched a bit, for dealing with our financial problems in an era of uncertainty.

The Parable Applied

The Hero is "Joseph A. Everyman," who symbolizes middle-class working Americans. The Hydra is a mix of all the financial challenges Joe must try to conquer.

Here is a summary of his major financial challenges: a list of the Hydra's heads. Check off the ones that apply to you (and, if you can endure seeing the numbers on paper, note what you pay for each in a month):

[ ] _____ Monthly rent or mortgage payment

[ ] _____ Monthly car payment

[ ] _____ College or graduate school loans

[ ] _____ Credit card payments or "rollover" debt

[ ] _____ Insurance: homeowner's, automobile

[ ] _____ Insurance: medical, dental, life, disability

[ ] _____ Living expenses: food, clothes, consumables

[ ] _____ Utilities: electricity, gas, water, phone(s)

[ ] _____ Luxuries: gym membership, cable TV, Internet

[ ] _____ Building a "rainy-day" or emergency fund

[ ] _____ Automobile gas, oil, and maintenance

[ ] _____ Travel and commuting expenses (parking, tolls)

[ ] _____ Entertainment (just a movie if one has time?)

[ ] _____ Saving for retirement

[ ] _____ Saving for children's college

[ ] _____ Assisting with parents' nursing home expenses

[ ] _____ Religious or other charitable contributions?

    $ _____ **Grand Total**

Usually there are others—new tires for the car, air travel to see sick Dad—which are episodic and often come as a surprise; but this list includes most of the Financial Hydra's many heads.

So Joe gamely goes up against the Hydra. He swings his sword—pays off Mortgage this month—and lops off one of its heads...temporarily. But up pops Car Inspection, which mandates new tires: find an extra $300.^{00}, quick!

He swings his sword again—pays off Utilities—but up pops Braces on His Pre-Teen's Teeth: find $300.^{00} more and contract to pay the remaining $3,300.^{00} in installments, quick!

Feeling like Jackie Chan with a rapier, he swooshes back and forth ferociously, and "kills"—at least for the next month—three Credit Card bills, paying *more*, thank God, than the Minimum Due. But Christmas is coming and The Wife wants (rightly) a bigger budget for presents than the pittance Joe has been allowing for birthdays.

Where's he to find an extra $300.^{00} this time?

Is it becoming clear why marriage counselors find that one cause of marital stress for *many* couples is fights over money?

When they married, Mr. and Mrs. Everyman had big dreams. Now, they have the daily morning nightmare: rush to find car keys and get the kids to day-care. Or if she stays home, while the baby naps she daydreams about a *new* car and a *real* vacation.

He is tiring of swinging the sword. She is tiring of the Dragon still breathing down their necks.

It is also clear that he needs to change his tactics.

Insanity or Amnesia?

When the Hero fought the Hydra, he wasted tremendous energy as he leapt back and forth lunging at one head, impaling a second, slicing off a third—even as he dodged the other heads. If the fight went longer than about three rounds, the normal hero would drop from exhaustion!

He had to find a better way to kill the beast!

Turn to our modern Joe Everyman. To generate more income, he leaps to a second Job: less time with wife and child, but at least this second "sword" permits him to "chop off" a few more "dragon heads" by paying some more bills.

So he pays off a VISA debt of $1,540$^{.00}$; but his oldest is entering college and he signs up for a $4,000$^{.00}$ tuition loan. He is now $2,460$^{.00}$ *deeper* in debt!

Worry, stress, frustration mount. And what if Job #2 is not enough to kill the Hydra? He takes Job #3: grab a third "sword"—trade what time is left for a bit more money.

One of the local bank tellers in my town has three jobs! He works at the bank from 8:30 a.m. to 2:00 p.m., manages a store part-time from 3:00 to 10:00 p.m., and on weekends has an assistant-manager position at another store...on his "days off!"

Is he killing the Hydra, or is it killing him?

One description of "insanity" is this: a person is insane if he keeps doing, over and over, actions that do not bring about the result he wants. Perhaps a man who works three jobs is not insane—it may be that he has merely forgotten what he wants.

The Uncertainty Dragon

The reader may think all this is too melodramatic, that *he* is a cut above the imaginary Joe Everyman. After all, he is a

Professional; he has a Good Job. And each month he easily cuts down all those bills as they attack him. College tuition is far in the future. His 401(k)s and IRAs are...growing?

But events in 2001 and 2002 suggest there may be a new Dragon breathing down our necks.

The terrorist attacks of September 11, 2001 injected substantial uncertainty into the Stock Market. And the sudden drop of the Market in July of 2002 increased that uncertainty.

In the fall of 2001, numerous industries shed jobs faster than you can discard emails by clicking "delete." Hotels, airlines, plane manufacturers, restaurants—all saw profits drop like a stone. They laid off tens of thousands of employees.

Thousands more from service industries such as clerks in retail stores were added to these layoffs, as retail customer volume seriously declined. Baggage handlers and airport cabbies lost business. Office and hotel construction slowed. Moody's Investor Service reported that in October payrolls lost 415,000 jobs.

Corporate profits were down 72% in the third quarter of 2001, compared to the third quarter in the year 2000.

Fallout from the attacks of September 11th spilled over into surprising niches of the economy. For example, some people postponed elective cosmetic surgery. In my community, a plastic surgeon's clinic had supported 15 medical professionals. In October of 2001, he earned virtually no income and started to lay people off.

But even if we could tear that terrible day out of the calendar, the American economy had reached a plateau. Apart from the economic disruption from the terrorist attack, consider these recent changes:

- The "dot.com" business expansion was in large part premised on the assumption, not the fact, that *any* Internet-based business would succeed. The assumption was not true.

- New "free trade" agreements have not yet benefited most American workers: their jobs have gone overseas, but the expected high demand by foreigners for American goods has not materialized.

- Many of the "new jobs" created in the U.S. in the last ten years have been in the service industries, where pay is less and employers can readily hire immigrants willing to work for relatively low wages.

- *Even "high tech" IT and computer guru types now run into the challenge of foreign competition*—a development so ominous, from a job-security perspective, that the topic deserves a separate section, based on numerous articles such as "Hiring of Foreign Workers Frustrates Native Job-Seekers," [*The Washington Post* (Feb. 27, 2002) p. E1]; and "India Rides High on Internet." [*The Washington Times* (May 13, 2002) p. A17]:

Now You See It, Now You Don't: BPO Sneak Attack

The shirts in my closet were made in places like Bangladesh, the Philippines, and China. Jobs in the apparel industry in the U.S. have largely fled overseas. This exodus has happened with many products. But the U.S. workers are still here.

But today it happens with services as well, with, as the *Times* article put it, jobs "that can be done more cheaply—and perhaps better—by some bright eager beaver in Bangalore, Madras, or Bombay."

The Gartner Group predicts that by December 2002, more than 80% of multinationals will outsource their IT work. *This is "Business-Processing Outsourcing (BPO)."*

GE, American Express, Citibank, Dell Computers, and Oracle have set up call centers or BPO centers *in India*, where smart, ambitious, computer-savvy college grads will happily work for as little as $245.^{.00} *per month*! In the U.S. few graduates with comparable skills would sign up at $2,450.^{.00}.

Hey, you high-tech guys! Wake up! No longer do you compete only with a man or woman in the next cubicle or ten steps away. Now it's also people halfway across the world who are willing to "bid" for your job at a price—salary—90% under your bid. *And low bid wins.*

GE, American Express, Citibank, Dell, Oracle, and many others are *not* "outsourcing" their business processing to some "technology corridor" near your city's airport—but to a high tech park near the airport in Delhi or Bombay!

What Happens to the People Who Lost the Jobs?

Here's a puzzle for you: "What do 100 local high tech gurus in the U.S. do, when they lose 1/3 of their clients?" It doesn't take a Nobel Prize Winner in Economics to figure the answer:

Everything else being equal, when a 100-employee business loses 1/3 of its customers, either (a) it cuts all their salaries by 33% or (b) it "downsizes" by 33 employees or (c) some combination of these.

To put it in very simple terms: either 100 people are left with only 67% of their prior purchasing power, or 33 people will have No—Zilch—Nada—purchasing power.

Of course, "everything else" is rarely equal. Maybe the afflicted high tech firm can enter a slightly different field…or find new clients. But in their search, they better not bother to knock on the door of the CIOs at Oracle or Dell *et al*—those folks aren't at home. They've already left for Madras.

And what about the individual 33 who were laid off? Most will pound the pavement to find another high tech job. Some will go back to school, to get that MBA, so they can re-enter a job market even further shrunken. Some will rush to start their own businesses. *Most will wish they'd started one last year.*

But until the crisis passes, they all will "hunker down" to make do with what money they have. Paying the mortgage becomes more important than buying many Christmas presents. They make the old clunker last another year, rather than buy a new car. They stop eating dinner out.

"If your outgo exceeds your income, your upkeep will be your downfall." Whoever coined this phrase was incisive. In a pinch, people reduce their "outgo."

But long term, the only answer is to increase income.

This book has two main parts. It begins with a detailed analysis of the financial problem. It ends with an analysis of an alternative income-generating system to solve this problem—the "Best Kept Secret"—and answers standard objections to it.

CHAPTER II: NEW VIEWS ON MAKING MONEY

Webster's Dictionary defines *oxymoron* as a "smart saying which at first seems foolish," as in *loud silence* or *jumbo shrimp*. One wonders: is there a foolish saying which at first seems smart?...as in...*good job*...?

* * * * * * * *

The last forty years have seen extraordinary changes in the way Americans acquire, increase, manage, protect, save for retirement, and transmit wealth.

In our fathers' generation, a typical family had one "bread-winner," the husband. Once children came along, usually the wife stayed home to raise them. But today in a majority of families, both husband and wife work outside the home.

From 1950 into the 1980s, parents summed up the preferred route to financial security in a simple maxim: "Go to school...work hard...go out and get a good job"—with a corporation—and work forty-plus years.

But the wisdom of that counsel is now in doubt. In today's roller-coaster economy, it is unrealistic.

In the late 1960s, earning and managing money grew more complicated. New magazines sprang up, such as *Money* and *Worth*, which attempted to provide tips on where to invest to obtain the best and safest return.

The world of attorneys and accountants admitted a new profession: the financial planner. Some sold products such as insurance or stocks, but others were "fee-only." The counsel of a good financial planner was well worth the price.

Social and Economic Upheaval

At the same time, sociological and economic changes, many quite sudden, increased doubts about the conventional wisdom. In the 1980s, with breathless speed, the computer moved from being an entertaining toy and professorial research tool into the mainstream of business.

Thus, besides the usual stock market fluctuations, overseas competition—for example, Japanese autos—the soon-to-be-omnipresent computer sent shock waves through the ranks of both middle management and, often, the executive class. Jobs disappeared overnight.

Late in the decade, major corporations seemed to vie with each other in a grim competition to see which could cut more jobs. Old reliable firms like AT&T, GM, Sears, Boeing, Proctor & Gamble, etc., cut employees with breathless speed.

For the first time in its stellar history, IBM laid people off. In a few years, General Electric "downsized" by more than 100,000 employees. The day Mobil reduced employees at its Virginia headquarters by a third, a Client of mine who worked at Mobil told me they, the managers there, felt betrayed.

Yet in retrospect they should have known: in a competitive world, there are no guarantees.

As I wrote in The Best Kept Secret in America, the "handwriting was on the wall": the computer will eventually perform any human service that one can program a computer to do—and the human will be out of a job. Indeed, *Fortune* magazine's cover story (9-19-94) was, "The End of the JOB."

The 1990's

Because of these and other changes, the 1990s were turbulent times in the employment markets. Gone was the firm expectation that the paternalistic company would provide security as long as one kept his nose clean and was—or appeared—moderately productive.

A mix of occasionally real and often imaginary prosperity in the last few years of the 1990s temporarily hid the fact that a basic change had occurred: the j-o-b market would never be the same: "job security" had become an oxymoron.

So the more adventuresome age 25 to 45 kept their eyes open for alternatives to climbing the corporate ladder. Surveys of students at leading Business Schools revealed a high percentage of them wanted to start their own business rather than work in someone else's. They still do.

Today, just about everyone in the corporate world knows that instead of working for one company for 40 years, he or she will probably switch jobs as often as six times! Many will change whole careers.

As we entered the new century, economic uncertainty spread with the collapse of many of the "dot.com" companies. For a time, everything had gone up; the cover of a major news magazine showed a smiling couple, and below them the caption: "Everybody's Getting Rich!" So it seemed.

The price-earnings ratio of hundreds of companies rose from 15:1 or 25:1 up to 200:1 or more—*yet there was no eight-fold increase in hard assets or real productivity*. It was paper, not real wealth.

When the "dot bomb" collapse occurred, trillions of dollars of this paper wealth disappeared. Woe hit those who put a second mortgage on their homes to raise cash to play the market. They might have done better by learning to count cards in a casino and play Blackjack! In a sense, they did do that—but did not bother to count!

Then the horror of September 11, 2001 intensified, at least for a time, the economic uncertainty caused by the stock market's slide and the job market's contraction. Many people finally grasped the wisdom in the saying,

"Dig your well *before* you get thirsty:" create a second flow of cash before you need it.

By November 2001, newspapers reported that over 400,000 jobs disappeared during October alone. Fortunate were those who had dug their financial well before the scorching sun was high in the sky.

Or, to recur to the opening metaphor: fortunate were those who sharpened a second financial sword before the Dragon came at them from over the horizon.

"There's No Place Like Home"

The earlier changes just outlined gave rise to the profession of Financial Planner in the 1960s and 1970s. The later changes raised doubts about the permanence of one's career, loyalty to the corporation, and reliance on only one source of income.

- The late 1980s and the "roller-coaster" 1990s witnessed an explosion of interest in non-conventional approaches to the basic economic question: how to make a good living? Many people concluded that they could do it from home.

- Some surveys show that 90% of all persons in the 25-52 year-old age range want to work for themselves.

- Other surveys indicate that 7% of the entire U.S. population is looking for a home-based business.

- In 1999, 15% of all purchases were not made at stores. Catalogues remain highly popular, but Internet buying and selling is expanding rapidly. You can stay at home and shop with your computer.

- Traffic jams in major cities are so bad that many business and political leaders promote "telecommuting" through the home computer as the only (partial) source of relief.

- Working mothers' enthusiasm for a "career" is waning. Many wonder if it is smart to pay a stranger half their net pay to raise their children, when it is now possible to work out of the home.

All told, to diversify one's income has become *essential*. People need "multiple income streams." Residual income is now as important to the "downsized" middle manager as it always was to movie stars, recording artists, and authors.

In fact, residual income is important to *everybody*: how many nurses and sales clerks would cut their weekly hours to 30 if they had an extra \$500$^{.00}$ coming in each week? How many attorneys would play all weekend with their kids, if they had an extra \$1,000 a week from an outside source?

Baby-Boomer Bust?

Have you come to grips emotionally with the fact that most older Americans will be destitute in 10 to 15 years? In his Internet economic commentary, "Reality Check" (Aug. 1-8, 2002) Dr. Gary North cites these worrisome facts:

- Between 1995 and 2005 the number of workers who are age 55 and above will increase by roughly 31%—from 16 million to 21 million.

- More than 33 million people are age 65 or above in the United States today. By the ear 2030, this population is likely to exceed 70 million: i.e., more than double.

- At age sixty-five, 45% of Americans depend on relatives for financial support, 30% depend on charities, 23% keep on working. Only 2% are self-supporting.

- Since their March 2000 peak, stocks have lost nearly $8 trillion in value, an amount equal to the combined annual economic output of Germany, Canada, and Japan.

- 75% of Americans 50 years old have less than $5,000.$^{.00}$ in the bank for retirement. *If they need a mere $15,000 per year to live on, this amount will last four months.* What then?

One wonders how many college graduates are in these impoverished groups of oldsters. If college is supposed to "prepare you for life," what explains its failure to teach the students the basics of success: how to build enough assets to achieve, eventually, both freedom and security?

If they ever will learn this important lesson, they have to read, listen to, and meet entrepreneurs who will teach what they themselves learned in the "school of hard knocks."

Financial Advisors: We Need One More

As life became more complicated, the ranks of professionals who help us with our money grew.

The Stock Broker advises on what investments appear to give the best return related to a measure of risk. But you first must earn the discretionary money to invest.

The Life Insurance Agent offers policies that can provide necessary cash to protect one's survivors in case of untimely death of the primary breadwinner. But you first must earn the discretionary money to pay the premiums.

The Accountant helps you count your money, determine your gross income and your "adjusted gross income" through legitimate tax deductions, and works up your tax return. But you first must earn the gross income to "adjust."

The Financial Planner, a newer profession, provides advice on asset allocation and long-term capital management, so as, hopefully, to maximize investment return (ROI) and consequent economic security. But you first must earn the money to purchase the assets to allocate

The Estate Planning Attorney assists clients to avoid Probate and to reduce death taxes legitimately by use of a "credit-shelter trust" and, sometimes, an irrevocable life insurance trust. But you first must earn more than enough money that is not immediately needed, so you can save it, to create inheritable assets.

Does anything peculiar strike you here? Obviously: *before you can really use any of these professionals who are going to help you with your money, you need to have the money!*

The professional will help you pump water out of your well, or to manage the water once it gushes forth, or to preserve it so your wife and children can drink, or to put it into certain pipe lines that the tax collector cannot rightfully tap.

But you first must have some water! Yet usually none of these professionals, including esteemed Estate Planning Attorneys, is an expert in digging wells and priming the pump—in counseling on how to create strong and reliable cash flow.

It seems ironic that there are so many seminars on *how to* manage your assets (which we hope you already have) and on *how to* reduce your taxes on them and on *how to* pass your assets (which we hope you have) on to your heirs—but *so little* on the *essential* prior question: *"How to I earn enough money—continuously—even to need all these experts in money matters?"*

To answer these questions, in the last thirty years a small but dynamic entrepreneurial class has emerged: what one might call "Income Diversification Consultants," or, perhaps a bit flamboyantly, "Financial Success Consultants."

It has its own manuals, such as Napoleon Hill's classic, Think and Grow Rich and, recently, Robert Kiyosaki's Rich Dad, Poor Dad and Cash Flow Quadrant. Success Consultants include a range of excellent speakers, from Anthony Robbins to Jim Rohn; and information/motivation publishing companies, such as Nightingale-Conant and Executive Books.

Best of all, as this book discusses later, good Success Consultants usually are part of a "Success System": *an actual, working business that one can enter and learn by doing and learn from example.*

To hear a sermon on virtue is good; to practice virtue is better. To hear a talk on how to pursue success is good; actually to *practice the pursuit of success* is better. To watch someone kill his financial dragon is good; to *work with him* in fighting *both* his and your dragon is better.

In an era when TV infomercials display buff and muscular "personal trainers" as they help less buff/muscular clients pump iron in the gym and get back into good shape, today there is also a market for those in financial good shape to help less affluent clients pump up their cash flow.

Everyone needs to find a "Success Consultant." Even if times weren't so stormy financially, even if "downsizing" did not occur, even if the Stock Market were not so erratic, even if terrorists had not attacked on September 11th, there is still the question: *How do I improve my standard of living and maintain it through retirement?* By which is meant:

Do I have enough on which to retire? Can I rely on Social Security? If not, what should I do?

CHAPTER III: JURASSIC PERK

> "Annual income, 20 pounds...annual expenditure, 19 pounds...result, happiness. Annual income, 20 pounds...annual expenditure, 21 pounds. Result, misery."
>
> —Charles Dickens, <u>David Copperfield</u>.

* * * * * * * *

Personal Saving vs. Government "Saving"

A concrete example will be helpful. Assume that when Joe Everyman reaches age 65, Social Security—if it's still solvent—will pay him $1,000.^{00} per month, $12,000.^{00}. per year. And assume he had a personal stock portfolio—private savings program—that does this as well.

To generate $12,000-per-year income through a private savings program means he built up a $120,000^{00} asset that consistently spun off 10% interest. Or, more realistically, he saved $240,000^{00}, that spun off 5% interest. The math looks like this:

Asset:	$120,000^{00} -or-	$240,000^{00}
Interest:	x 10%	x 5%
Return:	$ 12,000^{00}	$ 12,000^{00} annually.

This would reflect what a small *personal retirement account* (PSA) might do. It has some important implications:

(1) If Joe dies at age 66, *his wife and children can inherit $240,000$^{.00}*. Though not a great sum, this money is very important to them: it could well pay off her mortgage, finish the kids' college tuition debts, or tide her over some years of grief and adjustment.

In the Government "savings" program, the surviving spouse inherits nothing. Joe's "retirement fund" goes to other people. This result is unjust.

(2) If, after paying "in" consistently since age 22 and building his own fund to this point, Joe dies *early*, at age 50 or 55 or 60, *again his wife and children inherit the $240,000$^{.00}*.

With a PSA program, the saver owns the asset. With the Government program, all he has is a promise from Government, not an enforceable right.

(3) If Joe averages $50,000$^{.00} per year income over his working years, he and his employer would pay roughly 15% in FICA taxes or $7,500$^{.00} per year. In 30 years, allowing for no temporary job loss and no tax increase, he's put in $225,000$^{.00}. If he works 40 years, it will be $300,000$^{.00}. (This figure excludes interest earned gradually over the years.)

Using the past 30 years as a guide, conservative private investing would, through compounding, generate $600,000$^{.00} - $800,000$^{.00}. That's at least *twice as much*.

Alvin Williams, CEO of Black America's Political Action Committee, gives this example: A 28-year-old unskilled worker who makes $13,500$^{.00} per year and pays $1,674$^{.00} in FICA taxes could accrue $177,147$^{.00} by age 67 if that annual $1,674$^{.00} went into a conservative investment account that earned a mere 4% return. That would create 400^{.00} more *per month* than the Social Security system promises today.

For a widow who gets by on 600^{.00} per month from Social Security, to push her monthly income up to $1,000$^{.00} is a 67% raise—and in the real world, gives her economic dignity she scarcely had before.

Any Financial Planner who has his clients put their money into an investment which returns only 2- 3% over 30 years when he knows of other investments, equally safe if carefully chosen, that return 4-6% should be fired. Yet that's what Government does.

The point here is *not* that we should let everyone invest all his present (potential) accrued Social Security benefits in the Stock Market. There are other investment instruments which over 20-30 years often are safer: Treasuries, mortgage-backed securities like GNMAs, or simple bank CDs, among others.

The point is: Social Security is not the best way to save: you can't borrow against it during your middle years, you can't will it to your heirs, and *you do not actually own it.*

Jurassic Perk: The Threat of Extinction

Sometimes adventure fiction takes place in the prehistoric age—or, in a famous movie, scientists incubate dinosaurs on an island in our own time. This premise makes for passable if predictable stories. But dinosaurs are extinct, quite possibly because they could not adapt to climate changes.

We need to face the fact that Social security could become extinct as well, quite possibly because it does not adapt to economic and demographic changes.

The terrorist attack of September 11th drove the problems of Social Security off the front pages. But you will recall that a Commission, co-chaired by the prestigious former Senator Daniel Patrick Moynihan (D-NY), reported some months earlier that Social Security was in big trouble because, to paraphrase, *"In a few years its outgo will exceed its income."*

There are two books that serious students of this problem should read. One is The Retirement Myth by Craig Karpel; and the other is Gray Dawn, by Peter Peterson. These brilliantly expose the problem of "unfunded liabilities"—a hole into which every modern industrialized welfare state has dug itself.

Briefly, the authors show that governments of Italy, Japan, Germany, England, *and the United States* have promised far more money to retirees than they have set aside to generate income to pay those claims.

In 20 years the Government must pay out one trillion dollars per year to Americans over 65; so it needs over twelve trillion "in the bank" at eight percent interest to provide the funds to fulfill its promise.

Pete DuPont, former Governor of Delaware, in "The Lies of Entitlement," [*The Washington Times* (July 28, 2002) p. B1], points out the problem:

1. Tomorrow's elderly will be much larger because of the growing retirement of Baby Boomers;

2. We have promised retirees benefits that surpass those of prior generations;

3. *There is no money set aside to fund Social Security benefits except FICA taxes collected from current workers.*

Unfortunately, the U.S. Government has not really put any substantial funds "in the bank!"

To Cook the Books Does Not Fill the Jar

Imagine a down-to-earth example: you and your wife have four living parents. Assume that they, like most Americans, have no real savings at age 65 for nursing homes. So you and she—and your siblings, if any—must handle expenses. At today's rates, you might need $50,000 per year *per person*. That would be an impossible annual expense of $200,000.$^{.00}$!

Possibly your folks can "get by" with a half that amount. Still, to produce even $100,000$^{.00}$ retirement/nursing home care income for all four, you need $1 million at 10% ROI, or $1.2 million at 8%. Call this need your "unfunded liability."

Sobered by that problem, let's return to Social Security. The Federal Government puts "Special Public Debt Obligations" into a separate account. SPDOs are Promissory Notes. *The Government trades promises-to-pay in the future, for actual money it takes from FICA taxes in the present.* It "balances" the books by a "deposit" into the Trust Fund of paper having the same face value as the cash it took out.

This is all a bookkeeping trick.

To grasp what's going on, take a homey example: to save cash to take the family to the movies and buy all the popcorn and soft drinks, each evening Dad drops the day's pocket change into a cookie jar. In time, it contains $50.$^{.00}$ in coins.

Then, before they have a chance to go to the movies, a serious need for some quick cash arises. So Dad takes out the fifty dollars. Feeling guilty, he places a Promissory Note in the jar. It says, "Dear Cookie Jar: I, Dad, promise to pay you $50.$^{.00}$." *Now Dad can say the cookie jar is "fully funded."*

But Dad has not put an asset of any real value into the jar: no wrist watch, no gold ring, no cell phone, no silver coins, no ticket to the Super Bowl or Deed to the house.

And into the Social Security "cookie jar," Congress has not put, say, Deeds to Federally-owned lands or any actual gold the U.S. may still own. *When it comes to "redeeming" its Notes, Congress must take the funds from general taxes.*

As floods of "baby-boomers" retire, the only way Congress can meet its future obligations, is either to (a) cause enormous inflation by printing too much money, or (b) raise FICA taxes up to 30-35% of wages, or (c) push the retirement age higher, to 68 or 70 or 72 or 75. So Social Security may "be there" in 20 years but "there" is not where you will want to be.

If Congress does (a), how much use will be your monthly Social Security check of 800^{.00}$, if today's prices are double or triple what they are now? There is a powerful, though possibly apocryphal, tale from the era of hyper-inflation in Germany in the early 1920's:

> **A man entered a store leaving a wheel-barrel full of paper money on the sidewalk outside. Moments later, when he returned, the money was scattered on the sidewalk, but the wheel-barrel was gone. The thief realized which of the two would hold its value longer!**

If Congress does (b), Social Security taxes plus regular income taxes will take 50-70% of people's incomes! Working citizens can scarcely pay for their *own* grandmother; they won't stand for having to pay for *someone* else's grandmother. One doubts Congress would dare choose this option.

If Congress does (c), its treatment of old people will be the modern equivalent of the ancient myth of Tantalus, who was so rash as to reveal some secrets of the gods. So they condemned him to stand, hungry, under a tree laden with fruit—forever. As he reached up, its branches recoiled. The fruit was just out of his grasp—*for all eternity*, a sad fate for Tantalus…and for us seniors, as we reach for unreachable money.

Putting Money Back in the Jar

The Social Security Commission came up with some useful recommendations. Unfortunately, Congress does not seem open-minded about even exploring these possibilities.

Messrs. Karpel and Peterson are not optimistic that the Congress will put its Social Security house in order. Indeed, the former spends many pages at the conclusion of his essay, outlining what you and I can do as private individuals—not relying on dinosaur Government.

Not surprisingly, he omits the solution explained in the last half of this book. This omission makes his analysis no less valuable, but it does underscore the fact that this alternative approach is still "The Best Kept Secret in America."

CHAPTER IV: THE PRICE OF THE SWORD

The Goal

In retirement, the Goal is not to have a pile of assets. *The Goal is cash flow*. Most of us think the Goal is assets, but, even as at the gambling table, the chips are valuable only if the player can cash them in.

And we've been conditioned to believe that the only cash-producing assets we can afford are shares of stock—or, for the few who manage to finesse the down-payment challenge, owning a few positive-cash-flow rental units.

Whence come those assets? The conventional wisdom has been: work hard and, through vehicles like 401-Ks, IRAs, or one's own investment efforts, take whatever money is left after immediate expenses, and create a "portfolio" or "retirement fund." Call it a "Capital Fund."

How Big a Capital Fund Does a Retiree Need?

These Capital Assets will, so the wisdom continues, spin off cash. With luck Joe Everyman might earn 10 or 12%, or more; but in a volatile era, most people are satisfied with 8%, or—as interest rates drop—as little as 3% or 4%.

Of course, he cannot dip into Principal, lest the value of his Capital Fund drop by what he has withdrawn, yielding a lower return next year. Shrink the Principal and one shrinks the Interest that it will spin off.

This would be like a farmer whose food comes from his harvest every year selling off some acres to meet expenses—thus insuring that next year's harvest will be smaller. As he sells more land, next year's dinners will also be smaller. Sell too much land, and next year he will skip dinners.

That 8% return-on-investment is *cash flow*. That's what Joe lives on. If he earns $80,000$^{.00}$ per year today, he will probably need at least $70,000$^{.00}$ annually when he retires. His Social Security *may* provide help in the range of $1,200$^{.00}$ per month, $14,000$^{.00}$ per year. That leaves $56,000$^{.00}$, which he needs from other—his own—sources.

What number, multiplied by 8%, will give him $56,000$^{.00}$ per year? Answer: $700,000$^{.00}$—*far more than 95% of Americans have saved by the time they retire!*

"Well," you say, "that's not *me*. I still have 20 years before I retire. I won't need $56,000$^{.00}$ I generate; I can get by on $36,000$^{.00}$ plus the $14,000$^{.00}$ from Social Security."

Maybe. *We need to take inflation into account.* This is hard to calculate, because the "Consumer Price Index" (CPI) ingredients are "cooked" now and then, to produce a less worrisome result. For example, the CPI doesn't count *rising taxes* as part of the "cost of living." But unlike cutting out steak dinners and Bahamas vacations, Joe cannot cut paying taxes.

This essay not being a math workbook, I'll skip the calculations and jump to the bottom line: if inflation averages an annual 6%, then in 12 years all prices will *double*. That cuts Joe's purchasing power by 50%. At this rate, in 24 years, prices double again; by then his purchasing power will be only ¼ of today's: it's as if his income dropped by 75%.

So, if Joe is 41 now, when he is 65—that's 24 years—to match $56,000$^{.00}$ in today's income, he will need $224,000$^{.00}$: Mr. Everyman will need a Capital Fund of $2,800,000$^{.00}$ paying out an 8% return.

"But I have been saving for 20 years and I do not have even $500,000^{00}. How can I save two million more?" he asks.

Answer: he can't! Too much money went out for those little necessities like a roof on the house, food on the table, insurance on home and health and car, and (if he has children) that money-hungry Son of Hydra, college tuition. Worse, maybe he "played the market" as it "bombed."

If what Everyman has been doing for the last 20 years has not produced financial security, what makes him think that to do the same for the next 20 years will bring financial security?

If what he has been doing for the last 20 years, many of them years of strong economic growth and high prosperity, has not worked, it might be wise for Joe to re-think his whole philosophy of "getting ahead." He needs to go beyond trying just to save, and instead, as Robert Kioysaki recommends, *create a permanent income-producing asset.*

Create an Asset

The old wisdom was: "Get a Job." The new wisdom is: "Create an Asset." But not just any old asset, but an *income-generating asset.* Create an asset that is a "financial sword."

The purpose—goal—target—dream—whatever you call it, is a balanced mix of Freedom and Security. These and their cognates, Time and Money, are in caps because, like the Promised Land, they deserve great respect and should be perceived as a real, not abstract, possibility.

Abstract Freedom and Security equal concrete Time and Money: enough time to be with one's wife and kids as their lives progress; enough money to dispel worries and provide for their needs, including retirement for the parents.

Today the average Job will *not* provide enough Time and Money for these goals. Most jobs that do pay enough money demand 60, 70, 80, even 90 hours a week. Most jobs that demand only the standard 40-hour week pay barely enough money to keep ahead of one's bills.

The person who relies on a Job has only one asset: *himself,* his *own* time, his *own* work. He cannot afford to get sick...old...laid off...retire...take a long vacation. *No work; no pay.* The Job System is not designed to help us win in the battle against the financial Hydra.

A person can't be a Winner if the system he must work in is designed to make him a Loser.

On the other hand, the person who relies on an income-generating asset can—once the asset (some form of business) is up and running—*separate himself from its daily workings.* Though he is not there every hour it functions, it is spinning off income, some of which (after expenses) he can keep.

Change the word "asset" to "system." Create an Income-producing system.

Example: a real estate Broker sets up a sales office; he signs up and trains a dozen Agents. Assume that in a month each sells one house worth $200,000.^{00} at a 6% commission. That totals $144,000.^{00} income to the office. If the Agents get half, the Broker earns a net of $72,000.^{00}. If his office expenses are half of that, he takes home $36,000.^{00}. In a month!

The Broker has *multiplied himself* through the efforts of others, who have learned to succeed through his help.

Example: The local Orthodontist runs a clinic-style dental office with four young dentists doing most of the work while he oversees their efforts. He processes four times as many patients this way. He charges $4,000.^{00} per patient for 10 sessions: $400.^{00} per session, typically an hour each. If he pays his assistants $100.^{00} per hour, his office pulls in $300.^{00} net.

Multiply by four patients: a total of $1,200.^{00} per hour. Through this override he leverages himself through the efforts of the other dentists, who learn his skills and his success.

Example: A local plumber hires an assistant, then three more. As business expands, he sets up shops at five other locations. In due time his company generates strong cash flow from each and he is in position to stop working in the field.

Like the broker, the plumber has *multiplied himself.*

In these real but oversimplified examples, the "man at the top" realized that *he needed to replace himself with a System*: he had to "leverage himself" through the work of others. He thus earns many times more than 100% of his own effort.

In each case, the "team" he assembled invested much more time and generated much more income than he could on his own.

And finally, once the income-generating System was fully functioning, the "man at the top" could pull back, take a breather, enjoy more time with his family—*and still have money coming in;* this income flow builds his future security.

Granted, in the real world everything is not always rosy. It's hard to find good employees. During training they rarely produce enough income to cover their salaries and benefits. In a profit downturn the last guy to be paid in a small business will often be the Boss. And often, after the employees leave at 5:00, the Boss stays for hours.

But on balance, the small-business, multiple-productive-person model creates more time and money—real prosperity—for the entrepreneurial person than does the Job, where there is a built-in income "ceiling" because *there is only one man producing income.*

Outline of the Time-Money System

1. The Goal: Freedom and Security; concretely, enough Time and enough Money.

2. The Means: create or locate or join a System that can—granted reasonable growth—generate enough money and free up enough time in inverse proportion:

   For the person who owns or controls the System, as it produces *more* money, it gradually takes *less* time.

3. This System normally will be an asset of some kind, such as a Business—one which gradually takes less time to generate greater income. Unlike a Job, where your income remains fairly flat, in this System *as the time you put in goes down, your income actually goes up*.

4. This Business System will generate growing continuous income even when start-up efforts cease.

5. Ultimately this income should become permanent and residual. This is much different from a fixed-ceiling Job, which does not pay after you leave it.

   If there were, in the "real world," such a Business System, wouldn't you want to find it?

Ownership

Which is better, to own your home or to rent your home? Most people would answer: own. Financially, as you pay down your mortgage you build equity; aesthetically, you're free to pound a nail in a wall without calling the Landlord. first.

Which is better, to own your car or to lease your car? Most people would respond: to own. You'll take better care of the car and when it's time to dispose of it, it should have some trade-in value (again, equity).

Finally, which is better, *to own your source of income or to "rent" yourself out to someone who does own the income source?* Most people would say: own.

The reason: when you "rent" yourself to someone else's income-producing system, you are giving him the dollar value of all of your work in return for his giving back to you the value of some of your work.

No one hires you without expecting that he will receive more value *from* you than the cost to him of what he gives back to you. *When you work for someone else, you "build equity" for him.* So you produce more value than you receive.

This is *not* an "unfair" system: the Owner *invests* time and money in you to train you; he took the risks and tied up his time to create a business that you simply step into—often, for only a short time.

Then too, for the first weeks or months you may not bring in or handle as much business as he has to generate just to pay you! And he has some risk: will your honesty and reliability be all he expects, deserves, and is paying for?

So Marx was wrong: the employer-employee relation is not a matter of "exploitation." Indeed, sometimes the worker exploits the employer. (How many store clerks shoplift from the stores where they work?)

But, from the viewpoint of legitimate self-interest, this is not the best system for the employee: *it does not "build equity," because it does not build wealth.* **At the end of one or five or ten years, the employee owns no more than he owned when he started.**

He "owns" merely the conditional right to work there. This "right" depends on his health, his respectful attitude toward the Boss, his objective productivity, his willingness to "go the extra mile"—i.e., work 10, 20, even 30 hours extra per week, often without extra pay—and other factors.

But to look for...to recognize...to evaluate...to join...to persist in...an alternative, will require us to *break out of the mental prison of our conventional ways of thinking.*

Napoleon Hill was surely correct when he titled his classic on success, Think and Grow Rich. The operative word is *think*—in new, creative ways, outside the prison of old ways of thinking that do not lead to Freedom and Security.

CHAPTER V: "THINKING OUTSIDE THE PRISON"

"The airplane is an interesting curiosity, but it has absolutely no military value."

—Marshal Foch, French Commanding General
1915

* * * * * * * *

Brainwashing

A few years after the Korean War, investigative journalist Edward Hunter wrote an incisive little book that was titled Brainwashing. It revealed psychological techniques Chinese Communist prison officials used to break a man's will.

Hours of questioning…cells too small to stand up in…erratic sleeping hours…not enough food…forged hostile letters from family…these and other pressures helped them identify which prisoners would buckle and which would not.

Many prison camps had Minimum Security and Maximum Security sections. The guards threw the mentally toughest prisoners into Maximum Security. These men kept alive their dream of wife, family, home, and freedom. Into Minimum Security the guards threw captives who were fuzzy about their hopes, eager to avoid pain, or dominated by fear.

The tough ones didn't care about pleasing their captors; they kept thinking about escape. The soft ones could not see beyond the next bowl of warm soup. They lost belief that they could escape. They surrendered in their own minds.

Escape from minimum-security compounds was relatively easy—*if a man wanted*. Sometimes the obstacle was only a single fence.

But it was nearly impossible to escape from the maximum security compounds: a man had to outsmart guards, evade dogs, dodge search-lights, climb barbed wire, survive in the wilderness.

Surprisingly on first glance, *very few escaped from Minimum Security.* Defeatist attitudes and vague goals kept the inmates from even trying. Expectation of failure became self-fulfilling prophecy. *By not trying to escape, they ensured that they would not escape.*

But *a far higher percentage of American soldiers escaped from Maximum Security.* They kept Freedom alive in their minds, until a chance to break out came along. As a later cliché would have it, their bodies were "in the box"; but they *thought* "outside the box."

There is a lesson here for those of us who want to escape the rut we are in and achieve financial success.

"Thinking Outside the Prison"

The phrase, "Thinking outside the box," may have been overused in recent years by young Business School grads. I prefer "Thinking outside the prison." This is a more useful metaphor because of its implications.

When the topic is financial success, the prison is mental. It is that cluster of ideas, attitudes, fears, and assumptions that *inhibit* a person from imagining, much less taking, steps that would improve his situation or help him reach positive goals.

A classic example of a mental prison was the prevalent belief in the 1950s that i*t is impossible for a man to run a mile in under four minutes.* "Don't try it; you'll have a heart attack."

But when Roger Bannister escaped that mental prison and finally did break the Four-Minute-Mile, within a year a half-dozen other runners did so, as well. He changed their disbelief to belief. He changed their minds.

Another example: over 40 years ago a book titled <u>The Ugly American</u>, about a diplomat's experiences in Asia, described a small village where old women grew stooped and hunched from daily sweeping public walk ways with short stubby little brushes like whisk brooms.

No one had thought—"outside the prison"—to replace the four-inch handle with a four-foot pole, to create a broom!

To reach financial success in turbulent times like these requires breaking out of the conceptual prison that keeps us believing that we do not *need* to supplement our Job with an income-producing asset.

Here are some examples of causes of imprisoned thought.

Peer Group Pressure

Frequently family, friends, or fellow workers volunteer negative and discouraging comments. Think of a bucket full of crabs: some on the bottom grab the back legs of one above trying to crawl out and pull him back. They say, "You can't do it; don't try." For example:

- "That car accident damaged your legs so badly that you'll never walk again, much less run."

- "No one in our family ever went to college; what makes you think you are so smart that you can?"

- "That girl's got too much class; she'll never go out with you, so don't bother to call her."

- "The other team's runners have much faster times; the best you guys can do in this meet is second, if you're lucky."

- "Rudy, you're too small. There's no chance you can make it onto the Notre Dame football team."

Many people will cheer a marathon runner closing the gap in the last 500 yards; but few will encourage the person seeking to escape a rut job that limits his time, income, or freedom.

The person in a career or financial prison who, like the soldiers in Maximum Security, intends to escape, must pay no attention to the doubters who claim his idea of freedom is far-fetched and fanciful. Usually the critics are themselves stuck in Minimum Security. They don't believe *anybody* can escape. They're partly right: *they* won't.

Habit and Inertia

Because of habit, some people do not realize there is freedom beyond the walls of their prison. For example, last Mother's Day the local Safeway cash register clerk, a mature woman, complained to the author about having to work on that day.

"If you had your own home-based business, instead of a job, you wouldn't have to work on any Sunday," I remarked, smiling.

With a blank look she mumbled, "Uh-huh. Well, I'm trying to get assigned to a store where they don't make you work on Sunday." For all she grasped my point, I might as well have said "*Antidisestablishmentarianism.*"

The reason this good woman was confined—one may say, imprisoned—in her Job was that she had put up walls around her thinking. The only improvement she could imagine was...the same Job, but at a different place! That's not escaping. *That's merely exchanging one prison for another.*

Sometime earlier in life, she uncritically accepted the notion that to "make a living" she must have a Job. Probably no one had ever explained to her that *just existing is not the same as 'a life.'* Spending half her waking hours controlled by someone else did provide "a living." On occasions like Mother's Day, it did not provide a life.

If the only "prison" that bothered her was working on Sundays, then reassignment to a different store might provide escape. But there is no guarantee it would be permanent. Her day off would still depend on the good will of virtual strangers. Another person, probably disliked, still controlled her: the Boss.

People with "employee mentality" rarely break out of Minimum Security.

Flawed Financial Analysis

There are many financial mistakes we can make as we journey through life. But different periods in history give rise to different mistakes.

A few centuries ago in Holland the "Tulip Bulb Mania" triggered their equivalent of a Stock Market crash that damaged the country's economy for decades. Speculators bid up the price of tulips as if they were gold. But gold does not wilt. Tulips do.

In modern industrial societies, harmful financial decisions are usually not as dramatic. But certain mistaken attitudes about money can impact individual families rather harshly. Take the question of Day Care so the wife can work a full-time job.

Eighty percent of pre-school children's mothers work outside the home. But 80% of these, in turn, would rather be home. Indeed, a poll of 3,000 married and single women ages 18 to 34 revealed that a majority would prefer domestic life if only they could afford it. ["Return of the Housewife," *The Washington Times* (June 8, 2000), p. A21.]

Many working mothers do not fully grasp the financial damage they could be doing to themselves. Like a hamster running on a treadmill, their enormous effort may get them nowhere.

A prominent local financial planner explained their problem on his radio program; this is his analysis, paraphrased:

<u>Case</u>: Husband earns $60,000^{.00}$; wife earns $40,000^{.00}$. If their gross of $100,000^{.00}$ puts them in the 40% income tax bracket (including state income tax), the 40% tax on her income leaves her $24,000^{.00}$ take-home pay (not counting the FICA deduction). For her, this net is $2,000^{.00}$ per month. If the couple pays $500^{.00}$ each week for Day Care, they pay out *the same amount she brought in*.

Surely this is an anomaly: a woman works full time but earns only enough to pay someone else to mother her children!

The example may be exaggerated. Admittedly, there are thousands of variations on these numbers. She may earn $50,000^{.00}$ and, even after work-related travel costs, clothes expenses, restaurant bills—and those Day Care costs just described—net a few thousand dollars. Her hourly rate, after all taxes and expenses, may be above the Minimum Wage.

Then too, many women receive a good measure of psychological fulfillment from using their college degrees out in the "real world."

But if we run the numbers alone, and we omit subjective factors (whether her psychology or the child's), few financial advisors would tell a wife to expend so much time, money, and effort to net so little. And her "fulfillment" may not balance having to scrape ice off the car windshield in winter at 7:00 a.m.—day after day after day.

This case resembles the situation of some Clients I had a few years ago. He was a young doctor; she sold pharmaceuticals. They had a two-year-old named Stevie and a day-time nanny, Maria. Thinking about the math outlined above, I urged her to quit her job.

She resisted for six months. Then one day she called: "You'll be pleased to know I quit my job!" she said. "How come?" I asked. Her response: "One evening around six, as Maria was leaving, little Stevie went to the front door and waved at her—and he said, 'Bye-bye, Mommy'—*to Maria!*"

Sometimes it takes a shock to make a person realize she's in a prison from which she needs to escape immediately.

Washing Out the Brainwashing

"Brainwashing" is a strange term. In the Korean War, the Chinese Communists were not trying to *clean* their prisoner's brains; they wanted to *pollute* them—with fears, temptations to disloyalty, desire to collaborate, doubts they could ever escape.

To escape the "prison" of financial helplessness, the rut of the low-paying Job, the frustration of daily Rush Hour, the pain of the alarm clock, one must rid his mind of years of built-up "pollution."

The *idea* of the invention must exist before the invention. The *plan* of the new house must exist before one builds. The *dream* of finding a "New World" drove Columbus to seek investment for his ships. And the *belief* that you can attain financial freedom and security must dominate your thinking before, and as, you pursue that goal.

Doctors and lawyers thought that their profession would help them reach that goal. For many, it has; but unfortunately, things seem to be changing.

CHAPTER VI: TROUBLE IN TWO PROFESSIONS

"The tragedy of life is not so much what men suffer, but rather what they miss."

—Thomas Carlyle

* * * * * * * *

All is not well in the world of doctors and lawyers. Though medical and law schools are full, there are experienced members of both professions who will not advise their children to follow in their footsteps.

Physicians

To become a doctor is to enter a very difficult profession. The training is very long and hard. The public expects the highest possible competence. So one would think medicine would be most highly rewarded vocation. This assumption is not always true.

A man or woman expends tens of thousands of dollars to become a doctor...long hours...low pay...enormous stress during training...and little time for family life. Many physicians say that once established, the stress is indeed lower; but the income—which they thought would go up like a jet taking off—has hit a plateau.

Actually, in some fields of medicine, income is gradually dropping.

- Doctors have seen their reimbursements cut by 5.4% this year, even as they're forced to comply with a growing pile of practically incomprehensible rules.

- An AMA survey for doctors found that over one-third spend an hour on Medicare paperwork for every four hours seeing patients—*20% of their time with paper, which does not pay a fee, rather than with patients, who do.*

- Blue Cross and other health insurers routinely evaluate claims with formulas that cut doctors' income drastically.

A doctor friend of mine once stated: "Physicians working for HMOs make less money per hour than garbage collectors in San Francisco!"

One of the finest orthopedic surgeons in the Washington, D.C. area told me he earned $2,000$^{.00}$ for outpatient knee orthoscopy ten years ago—but today receives a mere 600^{.00}$. He is at the mercy of health insurers who insist on paying less—70% less!

Their rationalization is that a skilled surgeon can perform this procedure easily. So, like a successful salesman whose company shrinks his territory, this physician's "commissions" are reduced because he can earn them so easily!

As his skills increase, he earns *less*. Something is wrong here.

Some doctors feel medicine has become just a business—and somebody else is controlling the market for their "product." A few doctors feel they are in a rat race, and the rats are winning.

Besides health plans' refusal to pay more than a percent of what *they* assert are "ordinary and customary" charges for a medical procedure, many other factors cause malaise in the profession, such as micro-managing medical decisions by outsiders, malpractice insurance costs, and frivolous lawsuits.

Consider just the lawsuits.

Forty-two percent of obstetricians are leaving the Las Vegas area now that 76% of them have been sued— 49% of them three times! [George F. Will, "Lawsuit Culture" (*The Washington Post*, June 2, 2002, p. B7)].

Or check the amazing website, "overlawyered.com," its archives section from March 15-17, 2002, "Texas docs plan walkout."

"More than 600 physicians in the Rio Grande Valley of Texas are planning to walk off the job April 8 to protest the state's malpractice climate." In Beaumont, only one neurosurgeon is left practicing.

An article titled, "Doctors See Red," *Kiplinger's* (May 2002), p. 28, states that malpractice premiums are up an average of 15% just this year, and in some areas the increase is as much as 40% to 400%.

In Mississippi, many doctors are unable to obtain coverage because 17 insurance companies have stopped offering medical malpractice insurance.

More telling than statistics is the case the article recounts: Nicholas D., a Philadelphia orthopedic surgeon, who has never been sued, must pay a premium of $100,000$^{.00}$. He has dipped into savings, laid off an employee, and no longer adds to his pension plan.

Possibly this surgeon's gross income is high enough to tolerate such monetary bloodletting. But numbers alone cannot express the anguish and frustration that some individual doctors admit privately and sometimes even publicly.

For example, take this letter dated January 14, 2001, to a newspaper in a large northeastern city, from the Chief of Neurology at a local hospital there:

"My partners and I are practicing neurologists in the [named] Hospital System. For 23 years I have responded to care for the neurologically ill, at any time of the day or night and regardless of ability to pay. My group treats virtually all uninsured patients in the largest community hospital in [our city].

"Over the last three years I have watched as my *malpractice premium has tripled* and the *reimbursements have plummeted.* For a spinal tap I now receive about $45.$^{.00}$, *far less than it would cost to repair a toilet.* I am powerless against the onslaught and helpless to respond. The law forbids me to collectively bargain for myself, my patients or my profession.

"Two health-care companies control more than 90% of the insurance business in this city. *Far too often I cannot make the simplest of decisions without the approval of someone who knows nothing of my practice or my patients' needs.* I cannot pass some of the cost onto my 'customers.' As a result, my business is failing. (Italics added.)

"I, like so many of my colleagues, am distracted, frightened and joyless. Most of us despair that there is no future for us … no protection from corporate and legal Goliaths. Doctors now advise their children not to enter medicine, and are pleased when they choose alternative careers in which there is some semblance of sanity and fairness.

"This mindset must inevitably come to the bedside in the guise of a physician whose attention is diverted and spirit is broken. As one of my colleagues has said, 'We need a Moses.'"

The last paragraph's plaintive tone should not distract us from recognizing the economic prison this doctor and his partners are in. Unfortunately, *like a disease that has no cure, within the profession and our current legal and political thinking about health care, there is no remedy for his problem.*

To be fair, we should acknowledge that not all doctors feel this way. Many are quite satisfied. Others "deal with" the negatives just mentioned. But there are some who do indeed feel imprisoned.

There is a partial answer *outside* "the prison." Physicians who have problems like the writer of this letter should first admit the practice of medicine can no longer provide the time, money, and professional satisfaction it did for most physicians 50 years ago.

Second, they will have to find the time, and generate the money that they deserve, outside the field of medicine. An external flow of $50,000.00 to $100,000.00 per year can go a long way to ease pressures of medical practice. Not the least improvement might be to cut back their long hours. "Having a life" is much more than mere "making a living." One *can* kill the Dragon with the right tactics and the right sword.

Attorneys

If doctors are going backwards, attorneys now must sprint to cover the same ground. In any race, to pick up the pace is to increase the stress.

Part of the problem, at least in big-city law practice, is that many attorneys' new motto and sole focus seem to be *Billablehoursuberalles*. The motto means one must scramble to find clients to bill and then work his tail off to justify billing them a lot.

But running with a tiger on your heels takes all the fun out of running.

A survey of 125 big law firms found that over 82% of senior attorneys think the *experience* of the practice of law is "worse" today than 30 years ago. Only 8% thought it is "better."

The essay commenting on the survey added, "They work too much. They're under lots of pressure to 'make rain.' The competition is plain murder." ["Big-Firm Partners: Profession Sinking, *National Law Journal* (May 26, 1997), p. 1.]

Along with intensified pursuit of fees, the article cited other factors that convinced these senior partners that law practice is less attractive today than when they entered into it: e.g., less collegiality, and, among some attorneys, a fading sense of ethical limits. All of these trends take their psychological toll:

In an article, "Kinder, Gentler Lawyers?" [*USA Weekend* (November 26-28, 1999) p. 4] writer Lydia Strohl stated that "the profession is in a real crisis...Lawyers have the highest levels of depression...higher than average levels of substance abuse...high burn-out rate, emotional problems, and widespread disaffection." She added:

"A California Bar Association study found that 70% of the State's lawyers said they wouldn't choose the career again—and 75% didn't want their children to follow in their footsteps."

Should a young man or woman begin the study of Law today? Much depends on his or her long-term goals. If a person wants to imitate one those brash defense attorneys one sees in TV series like *The Practice* or be a self-righteous prosecutor like the lead in *Law and Order*, the answer could well be Yes.

But if the goal is to marry, have a family, and *enjoy a good measure of time with one's spouse and children*, one might well pause. For many attorneys, 60, 70, 80-hour weeks in the office are common.

If a man's wife has to put a picture of Daddy in the crib of his one-year-old, just so the child will recognize its father, his Job controls him.

No man on his deathbed ever said, "I wish I'd spent more time at the office."

One Way to Escape the Business That Owns You

Professionals don't like to admit it, but the practice of Medicine or Law or Accounting or Dentistry is a *business.* They might bristle if someone said they have "customers." Why, doctors don't have "customers"; they have "patients." Attorneys surely don't have "customers"; they have "clients."

Baloney! Though they had to go to school longer to get a license to enter the field, and though the relationship with those whom they serve may last longer than in other businesses, *attorneys, physicians, and the others have customers.*

They are, respectively, in the "Law Business" and in the "Medicine Business."

The "cost of doing business" has gone way up. In dollars, those malpractice insurance premiums alone have changed the economics of the medical profession—and, increasingly, of the legal profession. The intangible costs are higher too: long hours drain a person's energies and stress his family.

And to find customers, to extract fair payment from them for the service, and to handle overhead takes up so much time that there is little left for much else.

If Mary Everylaw, Esq. and Tom Everydoc, M.D. each is in a "Business" that requires 60 hours a week, they are at work 10 hours a day, 6 days a week, not counting time for Road Rage Hour. When is there time to do anything else? They don't own the Business. It owns them!

Tired of the hours and pressures—and because they think there is no other way—some professionals are back in graduate school to seek a new career. The current issue of my college alumni magazine recounts the stories of a pilot, a former pro football player, and two high-paid corporate attorneys, who are all now in teaching or child psychology or coaching.

The one drawback is—as usual—*money*—the lack thereof. In teaching and coaching, the former attorneys now earn less in a year than they used to make in a couple months.

There is no doubt that if professionals fed up with an unrewarding career could earn as much in some other line of work that they really enjoyed, thousands would jump to the new one.

Even more would jump out of their rut if they could fund complete freedom through a time-leveraged part-time business.

Why should a 40-year-old professional have to drop his income back to where it was when he was 25, to raise his personal fulfillment at work to a satisfactory level? If he then can't pay his bills, then he has merely traded one form of dissatisfaction—distress at work—for a different form of dissatisfaction—distress because of his empty checkbook.

Once in awhile, attorneys, dentists, accountants, and physicians pull back from the hurly-burly of daily schedules and pressured decisions, and ask themselves, "What would an Ideal Business give me?" Here are some things that come to mind: it would be a Business that provided more than enough money *and* time for

- Trips with the family: Disney World and beyond.

- Two-hour workouts in midday. Golf in midweek.

- Paying all the bills and then sending a hefty check to their favorite charity. Month after month.

- Paying cash rather than piling up loans for college tuitions

- Socking away substantial money in safe retirement accounts.

They even imagine how the Ideal Business could rid them of that monstrous invention of the Devil himself: the alarm clock!

There is a way to slice off all the Hydra's heads—to have time to do the things you like *and* the money to pay for them as well as pay for the necessities. The key is: to leverage a modest amount of *other people's time*.

Other people will be happy to do this if they are paid well for it.

CHAPTER VII: "OPM" AND "OPT"

"Whenever you see a successful business, someone once made a courageous decision."

—Peter Drucker

* * * * * * * *

Everyone who ever bought a house knows about "OPM"—using "other people's money." You buy with a small down payment of your own money and, usually, a large mortgage: other people's money. This is a form of leverage.

Less well known by name, but very widely practiced in business, is "OPT"—using "other people's time." Once a person understands the genius in using other people's time, he can move down the road toward genuine financial freedom. So we need to look at how widespread is the use of OPT.

Of Movie Stars, Computer Moguls, and Real Estate Brokers (Among Others)

What do Tom Cruise, Bill Gates, and your local ERA Broker have in common?

Answer: *They all use multiple outlets.* They provide a product or service through independent contractors who benefit from their collaboration with the named person and who, in turn, share their profits with them.

When Tom Cruise makes a movie, his fans do not need to journey to his home or office in California to see it; through an association or *network* of independent outlets—movie theaters around the country—the Cruise movie reaches its market. A portion of your $7.^{50} ticket fee goes back to Tom Cruise.

Because of his popularity, Tom Cruise makes money for the theaters: compared to an unknown actor, Cruise will attract thousands more customers to see a given film. Because of their multiple locations, the theaters (i.e., the owners) make money for Mr. Cruise: they are the only way he can reach so many separate markets around the country. It's a "win-win" deal. He uses their time and location; they, his name and face.

Turn to Bill Gates: he has assembled an association or *network* of skilled programmers and computer-design software engineers. Again, to buy Microsoft's flagship product, the current version of *Windows*, you needn't travel to his firm's headquarters in Washington State. Simply go to the local computer store.

So he uses a *network* of thousands of computer stores around the country, not unlike Tom Cruise's reliance on thousands of movie theaters. He provides an attractive, marketable product; they provide salesmen and an outlet, i.e., a place with access to customers. He makes money for them; and they make money for him. He uses their time.

In both cases, through a mutual-benefit working partnership, the creator of the product uses OPT— other people's time—to sell the product; and both he and they share, according to some wholesale/retail formula, the profits.

It works with a service too. ERA (or any other multiple-outlet real estate group you name) is itself a network. Here, let's consider just one office, owned and managed by Mr. Paul Broker, who has ten agents working out of his office.

Assume that Mary Agent sells one $200,000.^{00} house per month, at a 6% commission, which comes out to $12,000.^{00} for Paul Broker's office. Their agreement is that she is paid one-half the commission, here, $6,000.^{00}; the other half is kept by the office. Mr. Broker's overhead is half of that, so he nets $3,000.$^{.00}$ personally for the sale that took Mary's time.

Here's what Paul provided Mary: name recognition...office space ... secretarial ... training ... fax and copier...advertising...insurance...equipment...phone lines, etc. He provides these to Mary whether she sells a house that month or not.

Here's what Mary provides Paul: diligent field agent with attractive personality...increasing sales skills...range of friends, contacts, and referrals...*time* in the field showing listings, negotiating with clients and lenders, etc.

Like Tom Cruise through movie theaters, like Bill Gates through computer software stores, Paul Broker leverages OPT—other people's time—to create wealth *both* for himself *and* for Mary and his other nine agents. Indeed, if each of them sells just one $200,000$^{.00}$ house that month, he nets $30,000!

Not as impressive as Cruise and Gates, but then again, Mr. Broker has only a mere ten outlets—profit centers, independent business partners—whereas the movie star and computer mogul have thousands. But if the real estate market stays warm, enough for Mr. Broker to net a cool $360,000$^{.00}$ in one year!

In each case, the Agent is not employed by the Principal. He or she is independent. This de facto "partnership" frees up both parties: the Agent can work when she wants; the Principal need not constantly oversee the Agent to squeeze maximum productivity out of her. Incentives do that.

Make Money While You Sleep

The genius of seeking your market through a network of other people, rather than relying solely on yourself, is—if your network is more than just a few people—*you make money while you sleep.*

You can make money while on vacation, because other people are working. You can make money while sick, because others are healthy. You can make money on your day off, because it's some others' "day on."

If you have only one store, you have to be there all the time; and you do not make money while you're gone—or you have to hire a trustworthy surrogate and probably pay him most of the profit you would have made had you not been absent.

But Tom Cruise is *never* selling tickets at the movie theater, nor does the owner of a "chain" of theaters. Yet he earns millions. Bill Gates is *never* behind the cash register at the local computer store. Yet he earns millions. Paul Broker *never* sits alone all Sunday afternoon in an "Open House." Yet he earns tens of thousands, and some in his position do earn millions.

What do these guys know that you and I don't? Answer: if we've understood the lesson here, *they don't know anything we don't; they merely did a lot that we didn't!*

An Objection Answered

"But," you say, "Tom Cruise is one of the sharpest actors in Hollywood; Bill Gates is one of the smartest businessmen in the country. Moreover, *they* were in the right place at the right time; I am—in terms of talent, a vehicle, timing, etc.—in the wrong place at the present time."

You continue: "I don't have Cruise's looks or Gates' brains; I don't have an 'agent' who will get me good roles or a team of geeks and gurus who create 'neat' software programs. I'm just a guy with a couple kids, climbing a corporate ladder leaning against the wrong wall, middle aged, with an elderly Mom to care for, car and house and credit-card payments."

Are you done? You say "Yes."

Okay, here's the answer, in three parts. First, no one said you should go into movies or computers. All you need to understand from the Cruise/Gates/Broker examples is the *principle* of the thing:

The best way to make good money is through having multiple outlets.

Second, it's not just movies and computers; this principle is followed virtually *everywhere*.

- Bill Marriott has hotels—outlets, using other people's time—all over the country, and even the world.

- Tom Monahan or his successor has Dominos Pizza delivery stores—outlets, using other people's time—all over the country.

- Exxon and Shell and Texaco, etc. have gas stations—outlets, using other people's time—all over the country.

- Elvis Presley's heirs sell his recordings through record stores—outlets, etc.—all over the country.

- Ray Kroc's heirs have McDonald's hamburger restaurants all over the country and the world.

Third—and here is the key—*it is possible to get into the process of marketing through a network of independent outlets without investing more than $500^{00}!*

This is done through what one might call a "private franchise."

Two Ways to Crack the Income Ceiling: the "Public Franchise" and the "Private Franchise"

Obviously, unless a man is a marketing genius, to work alone is difficult. It requires strong self-confidence, discipline, unbroken good health, and other rare qualities.

For the same reason that solo law or medical practice rarely generates income for the individual as high as group practice, a person in the profession of direct selling runs into an income "ceiling."

He is "trading hours for dollars." Since he has only a limited number of hours in a day, acting alone he can earn only limited income. To this extent, he runs into the same limitations as in a Job.

To crack through the income "ceiling," he needs a better system.

What Wealthy People Do That Poor People Don't

Poor people and middle class people usually have one income source. Wealthy people build or tap into a network of income sources. The wealthiest people own whole networks.

- Whoever owns a television network is much stronger financially than the owner of a single station. And the latter is better off financially than any employee at his station.

- Whoever owns a "chain"—network—of newspapers is more secure financially than the company or individual who owns only one.

- Whoever owns a group of grocery stores or gas stations—networks—is, again, in a safer financial position than the owner of only one, and his net worth is probably hundreds of times greater than that of his store or station managers.

- Whoever develops a network of real estate offices does on a large scale what an individual Broker does on a small scale, with his network of agents who work from his office. Both will make more money—and eventually work fewer hours—than the solo broker-agent who does it all on his own.

- Lowe's and Cineplex own clusters of movie theatres around the country. How about calling them "networks?"

- All the big, widespread franchises are—you guessed it—networks of individual franchise-owners.

- What did Sam Walton do to become, toward the end of his life, the richest man in the world? He created a network of Wal-Mart stores.

To go on in this vein is not necessary. The point is clear: a superior way—arguably the best way—to make really good money without doing all the work yourself, and thus have a good measure of time—freedom—for "all the things I'd really like to do if I were rich"...is to build a Network.

So, the question is, How do I do that, without, as the saying is, it costing me an arm and a leg?

The "Public Franchise"

In the early 1950s, Ray Kroc got the brilliant idea that he could "duplicate" his successful McDonald's restaurant by setting up *identical* other restaurants and, because he had no time to be present there personally, sell them to entrepreneurs who wanted a proven business system.

Thus franchising was born. Kroc sold to others the right to run a new "McRestaurant," but he kept control by contract—insuring that the Owner had to follow his system—and he increased his income by taking a share of the Owner's profits.

Ray Kroc may have been a more brilliant businessman than even Lee Iacocca or Jack Welsh: He cut the connection between his time and his income. He used Other People's Time. He sold others a success system and, in payment for what they bought, he took back both a one-time start up fee and a small percent of their annual income.

When his own time no longer restricted his personal income, his own income potential was literally unlimited.

The key: *duplicate* a proven successful system. At first it was a popular hamburger restaurant. Soon others followed: pizza-cook-and-deliver (Dominos)...small oil-change shops (Jiffy Lube)...all-night convenience stores (7-11)...car-maintenance shops (Midas)...chicken (KFC)...more burgers (Wendy's, Burger King)...and so on.

How would you like to increase your income by 5% every time somebody else started doing what you have been doing? And paid you to let them duplicate you? Why, you might look for 20 others—and double your original income!

And what would your income be if you enlisted 200 others? Or 2,000? Or even 20,000? Joan Kroc does pretty well.

Soon the franchising idea spread into lumber and home-remodeling stores (Home Depot), office supplies (Staples, Office Max) and even unlikely fields like haircuts (Great Clips).

In most cases, the Owner is *not* the big company that sponsored the new outlet; the Owner is an individual who wants to be his own boss, raises substantial funds to buy into the company's franchise system, and ties himself down to one location and long hours making it work.

At first Ray Kroc did not charge much to buy into his system. But today, now that it is a proven success, the franchise may cost upwards of a million dollars.

Every single McDonald's you pass as you drive across America is proof that there are entrepreneur types who want their own business...who will pay a high price to plug into a successful business system...and who prosper because of it.

But the "public franchise" is not open to everybody. It has its downside: cost...full time required...and the fact that the franchisee with his one outlet does not share in the residual income that the franchiser regularly receives.

There has to be a better way. And there is.

The Private Franchise

Fifteen years ago in a newspaper op-ed piece, I coined the phrase "Private Franchise." It described a growing trend: a company authorizes ordinary people to sell its product or service as an Independent Contractor.

He is not an employee. He has no W-2 form. He has no set hours. He works out of his home, or out of an office he himself provides. He keeps track of his tax-deductible business expenses to partly offset income taxes on his gross income, which is reported on a Form 1099. He has no Boss.

At that time, there were independent contractors marketing college scholarship searches...fuel additives...cosmetics... cleaning products...discounted telephone service...pre-paid legal service plans...and a plethora of other products.

Unlike real estate and insurance, normally no license was required. Nor was incorporation needed. Some people dubbed this money-saving system "The Poor Man's Franchise." The term "private franchise" is not a formal legal term, but its nuance is accurate.

From the company's perspective, such a system is highly attractive: no salaried staff, no fringe benefits, no costly offices, no fixed salaries for productive and the unproductive employees. *The company pays the independent contractor field rep only when a sale is made.*

From the individual's perspective, the system is attractive as well:

As an Independent Business Owner, he can set his own hours, control his own costs, not answer to a Boss. He can work when, where, and with whom he wants. Because he has no set hours, he can follow his *own* schedule. Voila! Freedom!

This system, which began with door-to-door salesmen, still flourishes today. Because the entry fee is low, usually well under $500.⁰⁰ for start-up information, advertising brochures, self-training CDs and tapes, and attendance at an orientation meeting, *there is no real risk.*

However, in most cities, "door-to-door" selling is no longer practical: people are gone all day; many fear a stranger's knock and won't open the door; a dinner-time visitor is even less welcome than a telemarketer's call; winter can chill even the hottest salesman's zeal. Fortunately, there is a better way.

The "Private Franchise" Plus...

Almost simultaneously with the emergence of "public franchising," the pioneers of "private franchising" came up with a new idea. They created something extraordinarily similar, *but with an important 'plus':*

They created a business model that Ray Kroc did not need. The McDonald's company would set up person "A" with a restaurant, but did not allow him in turn to set up "B," "C," and "D" and earn a small percentage of *their* income. Sometimes "A" could buy a second franchise, but the residuals went to the company.

The private franchiser had a different nut to crack. It could make itself inexpensive: just license an individual to sell a product or service. Charge him maybe $150.$^{.00}$ and give him a Starter Kit. He's in business.

But there was kind of a Grisham's Law at work: as "Bad money drives out good," so inexperienced and amateurish distributors often gave a bad name to the less numerous professional types who got in.

Then too, once up and running with a visible building in a good location and curious new customers, a new McDonald's will start to generate strong cash flow. But an individual "distributor" or "marketing associate" works out of his home: he has no advantage of location and visibility.

Besides, the individual does not make much profit selling one bottle of vitamins, make-up crème, or discounted telephone service. Impatient people quit because they did not invest much to begin with and their mother-in-law told them it wouldn't work (something no one can say about McDonald's, though doubtless plenty said it to Mr. Kroc in 1960).

There had to be a way to bolster commitment until the profits started rolling in, and there had to be a way to bolster those profits as they did roll in!

McDonald's maintained the new franchisee's commitment by its high entry fee: if one restaurant cost a newcomer $500,000.$^{.00}$ or more to purchase the franchise, plus months of time to learn its system, he had plenty of reason to hang in there for the long term.

And once McDonald's was a proven winner, as visions of hamburgers danced in the new franchisees' heads, so did visions of dollars. They could hear the cash register clanging in their sleep.

But the "private franchisee" had no such incentive to stick it out during the dry years. The low cost of entry, a major incentive to "try it," and the low volume (thus low income) of his early forays into sales, could lead him to believe he wouldn't lose much if he quit after a short time.

The New Twist

Since the franchiser can make more money than the franchisee, the key would be: *Let everybody become both a franchisee and a franchiser as well.*

The pioneers of this new business structure gave each distributor or marketing associate—call him a "field rep"—the right to do the same thing *they* did with him: bring in another new field rep. "Sponsor" the next person.

The only reason anyone enters business is his anticipation of profit. The incentive is anticipated income. It's like farming: the farmer *plants* because he foresees the *harvest*, which in turn translates into *income*. Same reason a person enters law school or medical school. It is the Means to the End he wants.

The only reason "A" sponsors "B" and loans him business materials, takes him into the field to train-by-doing, spends his own time making a sale where "B" receives the commission, etc., is anticipation that once "B" does the business on his own, and makes some good money, "A" will receive an "override."

So, in return for giving the new field rep the right to do the same thing as the sponsor, the latter receives a small share of the total gross income the field rep produces—the same way as the McDonald's corporation receives a share of the income each of its franchisee restaurants produces.

A Brilliant Way to Protect One's Investment

It often happens that a law firm brings in a new Associate just out of law school. They help him with cases. They let him sit in on negotiations. A Partner oversees his work.

Some years ago, as an Arbitrator for the American Arbitration Association I presided over a large case with two lawyers on one side and three on the other. The experienced lead attorneys on each side could have gone it alone: the other three were there for the ride, to see how the savvy guys did it.

After a few years of apprenticeship, the young Associate is pretty good. He begins to wonder why *he* is not making the big fees the older fellows get. He never liked the Managing Partner anyway; he thinks the man is a curmudgeon. And he's tired of "grunt work" on weekends.

So he leaves the firm and, with a couple others of like mind, sets up his own firm. *His former firm created its own competition.* **And if the now-independent Associate is really good, he may come back, in Court, to haunt the firm he left.**

Don't think that this phenomenon is limited to lawyers. It happens in insurance…financial planning…real estate.

If Paul Broker, who owns the PB Real Estate Office, trains newcomer Mary Agent in how to prospect, market, close, etc., what will Mary do once she's well established?

You guessed it. In many cases, Mary Agent will leave and…

With a couple others of like mind, she sets up her own office. Once again, the firm created its own competition.

The departure of the young attorney and young real estate agent from their respective firms sometimes causes hard feelings. Also, now and then they pull clients away in their wake. So the firms lose the future income their young associates would have brought in and the potential income from the firm's present clients that they "steal" as they leave.

But if one is working with a good company, such an unhappy state of affairs does not happen in an association of private franchises.

The "private franchise" coupled with networking does not have this problem. The sponsor and the field reps are connected, in an informal partnership, by contract. The field reps' income is a share of the gross profit; the sponsor's income is a smaller share.

The field rep does not "leave and set up his own firm," as, in the examples above, the attorney and real estate agent did. He can set others up in business, but he does not first leave. When he in turn sponsors someone, he does not "create his own competition," *he expands his own business* by setting up outlets in other parts of the city, the state, or the country.

The Ideal Business

Let's fantasize a bit about the Perfect Business. Imagine its elements. Remember, the unspoken premise is: not only do we want Time and Money "someday," *we need Time and Money right now, while we work to set up that Income-Producing Asset for "someday."* Note how each of these elements frees a person up and saves/earns him more money.

1. **No Boss.** Work for yourself. No worries about layoffs, corporate politics, or martinet-type superiors who enjoy making you suffer.

2. **No Big "Capital Investment."** Start for under $500.$^{.00}$. No need to go into debt or spend all your savings.

3. **Home-Based.** No office rent. No rush hour. No wasted time and money driving and parking. No "road rage" or stress.

4. **Flexible Hours.** As little as six to ten per week, often in small one- and two-hour segments, mostly lunch hour, evenings, and weekends. Fits anybody's schedule, no matter the demands of his regular work.

5. **No Exams or Years of Training.** Unlike insurance, real estate, law, accounting, and medicine, the Ideal Business has token licensing at most and little or no mandatory expensive formal training.

6. **Tax Benefits.** The few on-going expenses of this business are mostly tax-deductible, unlike the costs of being an employee.

7. **No Discrimination.** Unlike a Job, promotions and higher wages are here based solely on performance, not sex, color, nepotism, or office politics.

8. **No Employees.** Thus no FICA, no FUTA, no paperwork for employees, no fringe benefits to fund, no trumped-up discrimination suits, no headaches when they don't show or they pilfer the cash register.

9. **Constant Strong Demand for the Product(s) or Service(s).** As J. Paul Getty stated years ago, the Ideal Business is one where you sell a product or service that people want, need, and can afford, and preferably this demand repeats again and again.

10. **No Special Sales Skills or Prior Experience Needed.** The Business is deliberately designed to be easy for people who don't like, or have no experience in, selling or any other aspect of business.

11. **A Senior Associate Who Accelerates Your Learning:** a mentor, this person offers continual guidance and has a financial stake in your success.

12. **A Time-Compounding System That Brings In Strong Residual Income.** By setting up a franchise-like group of "marketing associates" on whose sales one receives overrides, one generates income through helping others; in a few years, it comes in automatically.

13. **No Accounts Receivable and Collection Headaches.** The Business is structured to insure that the company you work with pays you directly, as soon as it receives payment from the customer.

14. **Minimal Legal Liability.** No employees means no worries about "vicarious liability," viz., an employee on a business errand hits someone and you, the employer, are sued.

15. **Unlimited Income Potential.** Unlike a Job, which pays only the price of replacing you with a willing substitute—and thus severely limits your income potential—the Ideal Business has *no* ceiling: income is *not* restricted to the efforts of only one person.

A Moment of Serious Reflection

Take a bit of time and go back over this "Ideal Business" section. Ask how much income you earn in your current Job and how much time you spend to bring that money home in daily expenses like travel and meals.

Consider today's economy: is that Job secure? Even if it is, what are your *real* prospects for increasing your pay at that Job by, say, 25% more.

Then compare the freedom and security you could develop through a Business such as we have just described. What we have outlined is not a fantasy. It is a real opportunity for any open-minded and ambitious person.

There is such a Business. There are people who, right now, are earning more money in less time at their part-time Business than they once earned at their full-time Job.

But as Tarzan swings through the jungle, he has enough sense not to let go of vine 'A' until he has a good grip on vine 'B'. Otherwise he could fall into the river with the alligators—or, here, with the financial Hydra—looking for a meal.

So the lesson is: one never quits his j-o-b until he has at least positioned himself to generate just as much income in his part-time business as the j-o-b gave him.

CHAPTER VIII: SET THE RECORD STRAIGHT

"Don't confuse me with the facts."

* * * * * * * *

Anyone who looks at a private franchising/sponsoring program runs into a few standard objections. The fair-minded person will stay around to hear the facts.

A Legal Triangle Table

Assume Mr. Mark Critic, an imaginary person, raises the objection. With a touch of miffed superiority because he thinks he's shot a sharp rhetorical arrow, he declares that the business is a "pyramid." To him, this means "illegal."

But just because Mark's arrow has pinned a label does not mean that he hit the target. To decide whether it hits, one should investigate whether he aimed at the right target.

First, before you fire back, it might be fun to remind Mark that he graduated from Michigan, spent three years in the U.S. Army, got an MBA at Stanford, worked a few years in California State Government, and is now a marketing manager for Wal-Mart.

Point out to Critic that the university, the Army, grad school, state government, and Wal-Mart are all legal but all are shaped just like pyramids.

A triangle—or a "pyramid"—is the natural form or table of organization of most enterprises: One person at the top; a few immediate subordinates (Senior VPs), more middle-rank people (Junior VPs); dozens or hundreds or even thousands on lower levels, fanning out more widely as you go down.

If *all* "pyramids" are illegal, it ill befits a smart and honest fellow like Mark to criticize this venture, when he's spent his adult life studying, soldiering, or working in various pyramids!

Second, the FTC and the Attorneys General of all 50 States know how to distinguish between the genuine and the counterfeit. They have had half a century to check out this form of marketing. They have approved its structure in general and the specific well-established businesses in it.

Third, compare any of these conventional institutions. How does a middle manager at Wal-Mart rise to Junior VP, or the latter ascend to become one of the (fewer) Senior VPs, and any of these finally make it to President? Only by taking the job of the guy above him, who must die, retire, get fired, or quit—in order to make "space" for the ambitious climber.

And even then, the "board" or a "search committee" may decide on an outsider—"We need new blood"—and give *him* the job the VP coveted for a decade. This means they give him the *extra income* VP expected and—quite possibly—deserved.

"Win-Win Partnerships"

Mark has a veritable quiver full of arrows. He fires another: "I don't want to offer this to my friends because I don't want to use people." Consider how off the mark this statement is:

- Does the corporation Mark works for "use" him?

- If a real estate broker engages, trains, and assists a new agent, does he "use" that agent?

- Do State Farm, Allstate, etc., "use" their field agents?

- Does a college "use" its professors and students or a hospital "use" its doctors?

- Do McDonald's, Dominos, and thousands of other successful franchisers "use" their franchisees? If so, *then why do people stand in line for months and pay huge fees to become a franchisee—just to be "used?"*

One could go on, but the idea is clear: these are all forms of *working partnerships*. People want the advantages of having a *mentor* show them how to do it and of working in a proven system and of leveraging the capital investment and prestige of the mentor company to their *own* benefit.

When someone offers Mark a solid and legal "private franchise," he offers to help him start his own business...to help with the business...to dispel his ignorance with the sponsor's knowledge...to bear some of his start-up costs...even to find customers.

He offers thousands of dollars of free consultation. So the shoe is on the other foot: when Mark takes him up on his offer, it seems that Mark is "using" him—except for the fact that *this is not a relationship of exploitation; it is one of cooperation*. A "working partnership" between two people who want mutual success is a win-win deal.

Now there are *two* people working to put Mark's son through college, put food on his table, pay his rent, and create a retirement fund for him: *Mark and his Sponsor*. If the Hero in his battle with the Hydra were joined by another Knight who would help him fight, wouldn't the Hero be relieved?

A "Real" Business?

Mark puts another arrow in his bow. He says he wants a "real business," and that this method of earning income does not rise to that level.

I control the temptation to ask, "How would *you* know—you've never run any business." Not wanting to be rude, I merely ask how a "real" business differed from one with the

15 characteristics mentioned just earlier. The skeptic will then say: a "real" business has employees...capital improvements like buildings...equipment...products...etc.

Yes and No. These are indeed the marks of *many* businesses, the good ones like Exxon and Wal-Mart, and even the not-so-good ones like Enron and Global Crossing. But all this is *not* the *essence* of a "real business."

J. Paul Getty, at one time reputed to be the richest man in the world, boiled it down succinctly:

A good business is one that sells to the public (a) a useful or valuable product or service (b) that they need or want and can afford, (c) at a competitive price.

Notice: Getty did not say, "A good or 'real' business is one which has hundreds of employees, has heavy debt, and has sunk millions of dollars into buildings and equipment." He did not get rich by looking for ways to pile up *expenses*.

It is *net income*, not gross "outgo," that determines whether your business is good.

Are U.S. Airways and United Airlines "real" businesses? Well, yes, but not because they own lots of planes, computers, and hangers; not because they have thousands of employees. For whatever reason, they allowed outgo, including debt service, to exceed income. Are they "good" businesses? Not right now!

And on the small scale that you and I might start a business, Getty's principle remains especially good advice. We might not do something as dramatic as grounding two dozen Boeing 737s and laying off 7,000 employees. But we must keep our purpose fixed firmly in mind: *Employees and equipment and buildings are a <u>means</u> and the Goal is <u>net income</u>.*

Indeed, since the more employees, equipment, and buildings the less net income, the strategy should be to structure your business in a way that you reduce overhead just as you raise income. The goal: low overhead but high income.

Thomas Jefferson famously said, "The Government which governs least governs best." One could paraphrase: "The Business which 'overheads' the least profits the most."

In a good private franchise business, there is no "capital investment"; no separate office—work at home; no new equipment; no employees. The out-of-pocket costs are trivial.

If a man or woman earns $50,000 to $500,000 per year in his business and expends, say, $6,000 per year in operating expenses, does he have a "real" business? *Certainly the money in his checking account is real!*

"Show Me (Who Makes) the Money"

Mark does not give up easily. He fires another arrow: "Only the guy at the top makes any real money." When I hear this, I wonder whether the critic has studied the compensation plan or discussed the matter with anyone "in the middle" levels.

On first glance, the critic could describe just about every corporation in the same terms: its president earns more in a month than the mailroom clerk does in a year. But there's a more telling rebuttal: *There are plenty of people on various "middle" levels who* do *make "real" money.*

That Lee Iacocca at Chrysler and Jack Welch at GE earned millions does not detract from the "real-ness" of Senior VP X earning $200,000 or Senior Manager Y earning $100,000$^{.00}$. It is a strange argument against working at Chrysler or GE on these levels because your generous salary is not as big as that of the man on the top level.

The same is true in a network business: the fact that a few "heavy hitters" at the "top" earn a million dollars a year does not detract from the freedom and security earned by those of less success, who earn perhaps $500.^{00} or $1,000.^{00} per month or as much as a "mere" hundred thousand a year.

Most working Moms would quit and come home from their j-o-b, if they could generate a consistent $500.^{00} per month from home. Most Dads who work two jobs, to keep cutting off those many Hydra heads, could quit one if they could generate merely $1,000.^{00}-$2,000.^{00} a month from home.

To Mom and Dad, these numbers are "real money." Why get hung up on the fact that someone else, who has worked at this a few years, makes 10 or 20 times as much? Would Joe Everyman refuse to work as a high-paid programmer at Microsoft just because Bill Gates "makes the 'real' money?"

Let's toss out that word "real." *Even if some other Knight has a bigger sword, the sword Joe can get his hands on is "real" if it enables him to slay the Dragon attacking his family.* No sense in being paralyzed with envy at other Knights' bigger swords while the Dragon comes closer

The Good, the Bad, and the Ugly

"I was in one of those things once, and it didn't work." Ever hear that objection? (You could probably say the same about your brother-in-law's old car—but nobody thinks to apply the same measuring stick to different vehicles.)

Consider similar criticisms of other undertakings:

- "My brother took me up in his Piper Cub when he got his pilot's license, but the engine failed and we crashed into a tree. So I won't fly on Southwest or United or Jet Blue or any other airline. I was in one of those airplane things once, and it didn't work."

- "I took piano lessons when I was a kid, but I can't play the piano now. It didn't work."

- "I sowed seed on my farm in March and April but there wasn't any harvest in June. Farming doesn't work."

- "I started a small graphics arts (or consulting, or whatever) business but clients didn't come. It didn't work."

- "I went through Law School and took the Bar Exam but I didn't pass. As a profession, Law doesn't work."

Ask the tough question: in each case, did "it" not work, or did the critic not work at it? If A, B, and C make some...or more...or lots of...or huge amounts of money in a given business, and X, Y, and Z do not, does the business "not work" or is it some people who *try* it for a few months who *did not work it?*

"I Want a Free Lunch"

A kindred complaint goes along these lines: "I was in one of those things once and I lost thousands of dollars." First, once again, one could say this complaint about *any* small business that a person starts but, as is the case with most start-up *conventional* small businesses, it then fails.

Second, some men and women attend Medical School or Law School for a few years but then, for whatever reason, decide on a different career. They pay perhaps $25,000.^{00} per year in tuition, thousands more for books and disks and study aids and Bar Exam refresher costs. They skip another $25,000.^{00} they could have earned simply painting houses.

The total expenditure (money spent + money-not-earned) over a mere two years runs above $100,000.^{00}. Yet when they quit, they don't complain, "I was in Medicine (i.e., medical school) once, and I lost thousands of dollars!"

Third, if a person understands the *low* costs of learning and building an association of private franchises, he wonders at the assertion that *anybody* could lose *thousands* of dollars. The books, tapes, seminars, fee for group voice mail, weekend training conventions, etc. don't cost much. If a person availed himself of everything offered, he might expend a few thousand dollars in a year.

Small price to pay to build a business that, for many people, *produces an income five to ten to even fifty times more than the dollars invested to build it*. The question Joe Everyman should ask, whether he buys a car or starts a business, is this: "What value do I receive *in return* for my investment?"

The problem many of us have is that we want the results without paying the price.

Anything worthwhile has some price.

In this kind of business, the price is quite low. In my opinion, the complainant has forgotten the "First Law of Economics": *"There ain't no free lunch!"*

"Psst—Hey, Buddy, Want to Buy a Bridge?"

Unabashed, Mark Critic reaches for one more arrow: the objection presented by someone Mark has never met, who offers free advice over the Internet. "I came across a website that gives lots of reasons why this form of business is a scam."

Yes, I have looked at such sites. In the anarchistic world of the Internet, anybody can put up a website that says almost anything. They remind a person of tabloid newspapers— though without the constraint of libel laws. It would not be surprising if a site somewhere offered to sell you the Brooklyn Bridge.

A statement in print is not, by that fact alone, true.

I am quite suspicious of free "advice" on financial success from someone who (a) is a pure stranger, (b) has no stake in my future, (c) will pay no penalty or suffer no loss if his advice turns out to be wrong, and I suffer loss.

When a man spends hours writing essays that poke fun at a business he tried for only a month, I wonder about his motives.

The Internet has many spammers, hackers, and virus-spreaders. It also has an excess of complainers: critics who themselves have achieved little financial success in their own lives and who have nothing positive to offer Joe Everyman to help him kill the Dragon chasing him. But they do have a site.

Why should Joe listen to cyber critics? If Joe wanted to lose excess pounds and build solid muscle, should he take advice from a website that lampoons body-building and weight-loss programs? Or should he talk—face-to-face—with personal trainers who are in shape and are willing to help him?

The tiny oasis of truth in the cyber critic's desert of allegations usually is that *he* and a handful of fellow critics who register comparable objections have had a bad experience. This allegation no one can answer: experience is experience, period. One cannot rebut subjective feelings.

It is possible to ride a popular roller-coaster...drive a costly car...study at a prestigious graduate school... work in a top-quality company...attend a "good" church...and sometimes have a bad experience. I know people who have. Chances are, so does Joe Everyman.

Or perhaps the critics joined a business program that was under-funded, or lacked a good training system, or did not market its products at a competitive price. Or, like every profession, even Medicine and Law, the program they were in had a small number of quacks and shysters.

Despite rigorous screening, now and then a charlatan or incompetent becomes a doctor or a lawyer. (Read the "Bar Section on Disciplinary Cases" in each month's state Bar Association Journal—and count the number of reprimands, suspensions, and—fortunately, rarer—disbarments.)

To paraphrase a popular book title, "Why do bad people get into good professions?" The answer is simple: That's life!

If a few bad apples get into Medicine or Law, we should *expect* that there would be a few in network marketing. This fact proves only that Joe Everyman should thoroughly investigate a program that seems to have merit. It probably does.

"Psst—Hey, buddy, want to 'buy' my advice on how to find fault with and prejudge every income-generating program that could help you kill the financial Hydra chasing you?"

"No thanks, friend. I already know that the *idea* works. This *specific* business I will check out personally with the people who are actually in it—not with an outsider like you. And, by the way, I don't need a bridge, either."

CHAPTER IX. THE CRYSTAL BALL

"Those who will not learn history are doomed to live it over."

—George Santayana

* * * * * * * *

People usually bring up this grim prediction when talking about cosmic social matters, politics, or the fate of nations. But it has an application to personal financial matters as well. From the past we can learn what to avoid in the future.

Myopic Hindsight or "20-20" Foresight?

A well-known saying has it that "Everybody has '20-20' hindsight." Probably the corollary is, "...but our foresight is myopic." Yes, the crystal ball is cloudy. But hindsight can sharpen our foresight. Let's look in both directions.

In the recent past we saw: serious Job losses...corporate downsizing...record Bankruptcy filings...aggressive foreign competition by technical types as far away as India...volatile stock market...low personal savings...mounting personal debt...rising college tuitions...shrinking corporate and individual retirement programs.

These are some of the financial Dragon's heads as it closes in on most Americans. And these do not include the emotional pressures: e.g., stress on working mothers; frustration in professions like Law and Medicine over, respectively, long hours and dropping income; arguments about all the bills.

If Joe Everyman sees these clearly in his recent past, what does he see in the immediate future—if he continues tomorrow doing what he did yesterday—that will make things any better? Will the future be any better? Or will he be "doomed to live over" the financially painful past?

The future *can* be better for Joe, *if* he will sharpen up his eyesight and look closely at what is happening.

The Computer: Use It or Lose (Because of) It

Who could have guessed, a decade ago, that the number one seller of books would be a company named "Amazon.com" but that it has no stores, even while hundreds of thousands of Americans can order books by computer while sitting in their pajamas at home?

Who could have guessed, back then, that in the fall, especially between Thanksgiving and Christmas, millions of people who can't stand packed parking lots and long lines at a cash register would sit at home at midnight and do their Christmas shopping by computer?

Who would have predicted that my wife could sit at home, sip her coffee, and without stress find hard-to-find items in a nationwide auction like E-Bay; or order all the consumables she needs—items as basic as cosmetics and toiletries?

Or that people who *really* want to save time could join a system of "automatic fulfillment" of their orders for these things, so that, without shopping at stores or even placing multiple orders every few days, they get what they need each month delivered to their door?

The computer has indeed caused the loss of thousands jobs. But it also created new forms of doing business: "telecommuting"...home-based profit centers... online publishing...website construction.

The computer has enabled creative entrepreneurs to set up *interactive* and *referral-based marketing systems* that interface perfectly with needs of time-conscious professionals and job holders who want to augment their income with a side business.

Because of the computer, there are now businesses that exist entirely on the Web; there are others which are partly Web-based and partly old-fashioned "brick and mortar." The founders of some of these had the prescience to add the "network" dimension we explained earlier.

They use a simple business idea: give to independent contractors a *discount* when they, as a "member of the club," as it were, purchase from this "webstore"—and a small share of the business profit when they refer a potential customer to their "webstore" and he in turn also makes a purchase.

Its as if, rather than spend megabucks on advertising, Wal-Mart "deputized" each customer to recommend its mart to friends and paid a commission to the deputy each time a friend came in and bought.

The final element that can transform this plan into a big money-maker is to add the "private franchise" element: to put it inelegantly: *deputize each deputy to bring in more deputies to do the same thing.*

I know high-income entrepreneurs in three different industries who have done just this. Clearly, despite the shocks to the economy in the last three years, not all is "doom and gloom" financially. To recur to our continuing metaphor: these individuals have assembled a group of Knights and given them each a sharp sword to fight the Hydra.

If a person peers carefully into the crystal ball, he can see that many people have their financial Hydra on the run.

To FIND OUT MORE ABOUT HOW PRIVATE FRANCHISING SOLVES FINANCIAL PROBLEMS, PLEASE CONTACT THE PERSON WHO GAVE YOU THIS BOOK.